HOME SWEET HOME
COLORING BOOK

TERESA GOODRIDGE

DOVER PUBLICATIONS, INC.
MINEOLA, NEW YORK

This heartwarming coloring book features thirty-one detailed illustrations highlighting the joys and comforts of home. From lovingly furnished living areas to relaxing outdoor spots, the sense of "home" truly shines through. Favorite pastimes such as knitting, baking, gardening, and playing music as well as the welcome presence of beloved pets add to the uplifting atmosphere. These delightful images will spark your imagination—plus, the perforated pages make displaying your finished work easy!

Bibliographical Note

Home Sweet Home Coloring Book is a new work,
first published by Dover Publications, Inc., in 2019.

International Standard Book Number

ISBN-13: 978-0-486-83757-4
ISBN-10: 0-486-83757-2

Manufactured in the United States by LSC Communications
83757203
www.doverpublications.com

4 6 8 10 9 7 5 3

2020